Transforming Loss:
A Discovery Process

Other books by John M. Schneider:

Finding My Way: *Healing and Transformation Through Loss and Grief*

Grief's Wisdom: *Quotes that Validate the Transformative Process*

The Overdiagnosis of Depression: *Recognizing Grief and its Transformative Potential*

Transforming Loss

A Discovery Process

John M. Schneider, PhD

with
Susan K. Zimmerman

INTEGRA Press ▪ East Lansing, Michigan ▪ 2006

This book is a condensed version of
Finding My Way:
Healing and Transformation Through Loss and Grief
by John M. Schneider, PhD

This book has been condensed and recast by
Susan K. Zimmerman
(in collaboration with John M. Schneider)
Graphics production and page layout by Jonathan Golden

We are indebted to a number of people who helped make
this book possible: *Douglas C. Bloodgood, Jeanne Drewes,*
Elizabeth Field, Mary Elaine Kiener, PhD,
Eldon R. Nonnamaker, EdD, *Kelly Rhoades,* PhD, *Barbara Sawyer-Koch*
and *Sally Smolen,* PhD, as well as many who have
so willingly shared their stories with the authors.

Photographs by
Douglas C. Bloodgood, Jonathan Golden,
John M. Schneider and *Susan Zimmerman*

ISBN 0-9772980-0-0

INTEGRA Press
P.O. Box 6013
East Lansing, MI 48826
517/339-7964
www.integraonline.org

Transforming Loss

*This slim book is a re-telling of
epiphanies & wisdom to be found in
Dr. John M. Schneider's*
Finding My Way:
Healing and Transformation Through Loss and Grief,
*offered by someone who has been sharing this process for
many years with people who are grappling with the changes
in their lives. But also, she has personally experienced major
changes and losses, and found that Dr. Schneider is right
in calling this **a discovery process** — one that can lead to
renewal and transformation!*

A Preface *by*
Susan K. Zimmerman:

*U*ndertaking the condensing and editing of this book initially seemed overwhelming as John M. Schneider's book, **Finding My Way**, was the most profound book on loss and grief that I had ever read. And I have heard the same thing from countless others over many years.

John's deep understanding of the grief process and potential for healing needed to be further shared. His years of research, his work with so many who were struggling through major losses and his own journey from grief to healing and transformation meant his writing was grounded in reality. For me, it was as if he had crawled inside my head and untangled the snarl of thoughts and emotions stuck there as I wrestled with huge losses in my life.

My husband died just past his 36th birthday leaving my young children and me with the necessity of rebuilding our lives. His heart attack six months earlier led to a "brain-death-vegetative-state" and a prognosis that he could live for years. And, all of this just after he had just been pronounced "cured" from the testicular cancer that he had battled for the previous eight years!

My 5-year-old daughter, 10-year-old son and I were grappling with the staggering practical issues – financial worries, house care, car maintenance and a pile of insurance claims to settle. The emotional impact of our loss was staggering and we each felt spiritually wounded.

I would need to quickly build skills necessary for rebuilding our lives, and yet my heart and mind were in a state of confusion. I felt devastated one minute and panic stricken the next. With no immediate family within 1000 miles, I knew our survival was going to depend on me!

Some wise voice deep inside seemed to say I would never make it if I didn't allow myself to grieve. My jumbled emotions, confused mind and broken spirit had to be healed before I could move our lives forward.

As I let tears flow, found ways to seek solace, and expressed my pain through journaling, creative dance movement, and talking with the few friends who were willing to listen, I began the long journey through my grief.

There were weeks of new, daily awareness of the depth and breadth of our loss, but eventually I began to gain a sense of my capabilities. I found confidence in taking on new tasks – small ones at first – but larger and larger ones as my self confidence increased. I began to realize that I wasn't the only newly widowed woman and young mother traveling this lonely path. This was a time in life when most couples who were in their early thirties, as I was, were busy building their families. My peers didn't know what to do with me.

As I moved through my healing process, friends began to send me their young acquaintances whose spouses had died. They were seeking people with answers for dealing with all their losses. And, thus, I began a program at Lansing Community College teaching some of the things I had been forced to learn, and giving them a voice for their experience and feelings.

There were women even younger than I had been, many with children in their toddler years – even one woman who was pregnant when her husband was killed in an accident. She would have to go through labor and delivery while grieving her husband's death. Eventually the men began to come too. Some needed to learn how to cook, wash laundry, and cope with other practical matters. And they all were hurting deeply as they struggled to find safe places to share their pain and sorrow.

It was during the early years of this work that I met John Schneider. He was teaching and conducting research at Michigan State University which led to the development of an instrument that measured individual grief (the R.T.L.*) Many of the students in my classes took this "test," thus helping to build knowledge and understanding of grief's process.

As John shared his findings and his model, his work spoke so clearly to me – giving clarity to my own personal experience, as well as that of many in my classes. His test results were so specific regarding where each participant was in their process that it seemed as if John had been present in our classroom for the entire semester – he had an understanding of each one's point in the healing process that would typically only come from a close

acquaintanceship with each.

As I read John's writings, I realized that I had been observing transformations unfolding in these bereaved men and women. I could be with them through even very dark moments because I knew the rich potential for this transformation – they would come out on the other side of their loss, finding new strengths in themselves, probably even making new discoveries about life. They would heal and gain new insights. Watching this transformation unfold was like sitting on the edge of a field of flowers and through time-lapse photography watching them unfold and bloom!

There are so many stories of growth and enrichment that I've witnessed – even sharing "friendship" on the path towards healing. Rose was a woman in her mid-fifties who was totally dependent on her husband while he was alive. After fully grieving his death, she began to learn to drive – something for which she had also depended on him. For Rose, learning to drive became a metaphor of encouragement for further growth and confidence. She said afterwards, "For so long, I didn't think I would survive this, but I'm beginning to discover things about myself I never knew. I'm feeling now that I can go on; probably I can even enjoy the rest of my life."

Jan, who was a young mother of a 2- and a 4-year-old, eventually went back to college

---

*R.T.L. – The Response to Loss Inventory is an inventory of the ways people respond to losses in their lives. (Copyright Schneider-Deutsch, 1994)

and years later became a psychotherapist, helping others through their losses.

Ted was left alone to raise his disabled 7-year-old daughter and her 9-year-old brother. He brought his children to the children's group that formed later, and found other families broken by the death of a parent. Ted said, "This is the first time since Sharon's death that we feel like a family again. Others there mirrored this for us – we are beginning to heal more deeply now."

As years went on, the class members and other bereaved people wanted more contact, and thus The Widowed Persons Group evolved – a place where these people could continue to learn, grow and give back to others.

My own work in this area of grief and loss has continued and expanded; I now work with people with losses of all kinds: deteriorative illness, death of a pet, divorce, and many other situations. I find that John's model of grief applies to all losses, even life changes – events we wouldn't necessarily think of as loss. This simple, yet profound process that John described, even discovered, certainly gave clarity to my experience and that of so many others. Thus, with a sense of awe over John's great ability to help with understanding how we cope, recover, heal, and transform from loss, I share this shortened version of his model and work.

I hope that this small book will speak to you in some way, maybe even being of some assistance as you face your own challenges and possibly those of others around you.

Susan K. Zimmerman, *President*
INTEGRA: The Association of Integrative
& Transformative Grief

Transforming Loss:
A Discovery Process

*The quotes that cling to the margins of some text pages,
implicitly commenting on or illuminating the topic at hand,
are selected from the many such quotes compiled by
Dr. John M. Schneider in* **Grief's Wisdom:**
Quotes that Validate the Transformative Process
(Season's Press, 1994)

Introduction:
CHANGE
AS LOSS

In today's world, there are numerous forces that are causing widespread changes – political, economic, environmental and personal ones. The 21st century began with powerful life changing events like the World Trade Center and Pentagon disasters of September 11, 2001, the war in Iraq and the tsunami disaster. Epidemics such as AIDS, environmental disasters, and the drug problem are several other changes sweeping the world. Added to these social and ecological forces are the natural changes, losses and deaths that are inherent in the growth and aging of individuals and families.

Change disrupts the ways we relate to meaningful parts of our lives. And it impacts the ways we experience, anticipate, and express ourselves. Typically, changes can be viewed as either of two types: natural changes or ones that disrupt our developmental process.

With natural changes, there are losses involved in growing up, maturing, and aging. Even dying can be seen as part of a natural life cycle. These changes include the everyday losses of life and death. For example, we lose the comforts of the womb, the closeness we had with mother as a baby when we are born. Throughout our lives, there are many losses that are normal.

Grief teaches the steadiest minds to waver.
–Sophocles, *Antigone* (cc. 442 BC)

Conversely, there also are many changes that are neither natural nor universal, but rather are disruptive. These include losses that are "normal" at one age, but disruptive at another, because they happened too soon, such as losing our parents as a child. Or they may happen too late, such as leaving home for the first time at age forty. Disruptive losses may also include traumatic, often sudden occurrences that exceed our capacity to continue life as usual.

Both natural and developmentally disruptive losses can lead to profound challenges to that which gives our lives meaning and pleasure. And both natural and disruptive losses will likely create a grief reaction.

Grief is the healing mechanism we have in order to deal with change. We grieve to make sense of the changes in our lives. Grief restores laughter, releases tears, and admits both delight and regret. We can find in grief, the source of creativity, love and renewal! It is a popular myth to think that only the death of a loved one involves the kind of change that warrants grieving. But, in fact, grief is a natural response to all types of changes – from everyday life changes to the overwhelming ones. Grief is actually a natural response to ANY change we experience. Whether large or small, change will affect us and create a loss of something and the resulting response of grief.

Perhaps most surprising of all is the fact that changes of a positive nature, not just those we view as negative, will also trigger a grief reaction. Something is lost or left behind when we create or experience a positive change in our lives. A new bride and groom each find they have left the security of old routines and now must adjust their behaviors to include another person.

Inherent in any change is both a loss and a gain. One may be more apparent than the other at the onset. We choose in this book to focus on the "loss" aspect of change as a starting point. It could just as easily have been the other way around, since even the most positive of life events include some loss. Most often, however, it is the loss aspect we are most likely to associate with the initial wave of grief.

Thus, if grief is a natural, even healthy, response to a change in our lives, we will find that we move through a process – a process which will itself change – as we absorb all that these changes mean to us.

Everything in life that we really accept undergoes a change.
–Katherine Mansfield, Journal of Katherine Mansfield (1927)

This process is a very natural progression – it is important to our full realization of the impact of the change – absorbing all that it means in our lives. It is a natural way of attempting to make sense of the change.

And, since grief is a process, this means that it takes place over time – rather than in one great moment of realization and completion. We humans cannot have a "good cry" and be done with it; rather it will seem to return time and time again – each time it may be triggered by a new memory or realization of the loss.

We've all heard of the "stages" of grief, but new research and understanding has helped us to know that this is not a linear process, nor is it comprised of static states of being. It does not require deep psychological understanding to move through the process. It actually can be simply characterized by three simple questions that we must ask ourselves. Questions that can help us to discern the extent of any change, its limits and the possibilities those changes create.

In their simplicity, these questions relieve us of the necessity of textbook-type study of grief "stages" and places the understanding of the process of grief in the hands of any individual – anyone who is grieving, or anyone who is supporting a bereaved person. And, best of all, there is a positive, hopeful tone in these questions, and in their movement into and through loss, awareness and healing. They actually are discoveries – discoveries that one can make along the path of grieving.

The movement from certainty to uncertainty is what I call fear... Most of us want to have our minds continually occupied so that we are prevented from seeing ourselves as we actually are. We are afraid to be empty. We are afraid to look at our fears.   ~ J. Krishnamurti, *Freedom From the Known* (1969)

The discerning questions are:

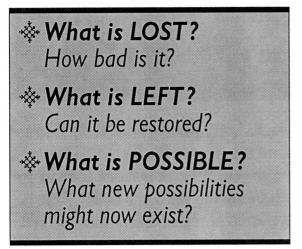

✤ **What is LOST?**
How bad is it?

✤ **What is LEFT?**
Can it be restored?

✤ **What is POSSIBLE?**
What new possibilities might now exist?

These questions serve to guide different points in the grieving process. And remember, it is a process – typically not something you can sit down one afternoon and get through. Sometimes it can be years between the questions. As a process of discovery, grief can serve to describe, express or alter what we are going through.

These three questions generally follow one another, but there is no hard and fixed rule about that. Often with positive change, for instance, people start with what remains, or has been gained, and only later go back to the loss aspect. Some people want to quickly get on with their lives, skip over the loss questions, only to again find themselves, perhaps half a lifetime later, coming back to ask and discover what was lost at the start.

If we move away from thinking of the process as consisting of the kind of static stages that came with the Kübler-Ross model of denial, anger, bargaining, depression and acceptance, then we can consider that each time a new aspect of the loss is experienced, we move through these questions once again – this time with a new meaning or depth.

Although these questions can seem simple and forthright, working through each takes time, energy and commitment. This work requires patience, understanding, love, courage and continued vulnerability. As we move through this process, we go from being victims of what has happened, through times when all we could do is survive by coping with and adjusting to the loss, eventually to the creation of new possibilities. These new possibilities could not have existed prior to this major life change – the true measure of an experience being transformative.

In short, the ultimate reward extends far beyond victimhood and survival (coping). Through these darkest times, healing can take place. Opportunities can emerge – for choice, for growth and even possibly new love. Fully answering these three questions as we move through the grieving process transforms lives!

Armed with your own courage, patience and willingness to be open, let us then examine these questions in greater depth.

What is LOST?

This first question involves sorting out what actually IS lost – the depth of that loss and the extent of its impact on our lives. How much of life has changed? What in our lives is no longer as it was? What and where are the voids, the holes?

As we struggle with the full consequences of what has really happened to us, we begin to discover the depth of our loss. Related questions surface: What have we actually lost? What isn't there now that was there previously? What is it that is no longer possible? We are discovering what is gone forever.

These are painful thoughts that demand much soul searching and patience for answers to unfold over time. The answers or discoveries can be isolating, causing us to feel very lonely. But eventually as we ask the questions and contemplate that which we've lost, we begin to get a picture of just how extensive this loss is.

Questions we may ask and which can be instrumental as we move through this part of our grief:

❖ *Has it really happened?* (Grieving Begins)
❖ *I can overcome this!* (Fight = Holding On)
❖ *Why face it?* (Flight = Letting Go)
❖ *How much has changed?* (Awareness)

This time involves the need to acknowledge that something is missing and to find ways to cope while gradually discovering the extent of the loss.

In following this path of discovery through our grief, it often begins with shock – a period of unbelief or a dream-like state. This can be followed by attempts to escape from the loss or overcome it. Interspersed throughout these behaviors can be periods of admission of its reality.

During the first weeks after her husband's death, Susan described her early grief with these words, "I'm still receiving phone calls from people who don't know about his

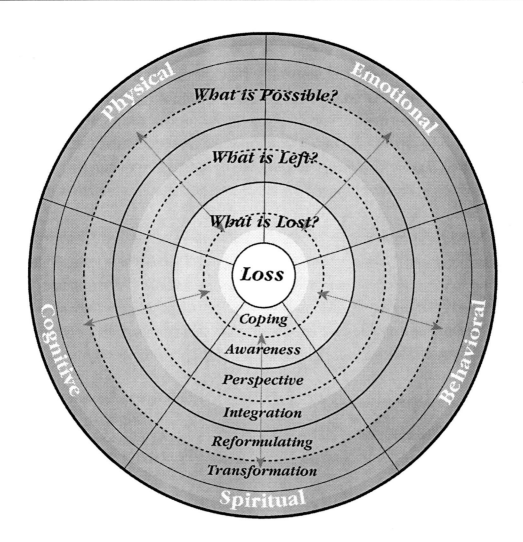

The Process of Grieving

"I consider grief to be composed of themes, or phases, which occur in the context of a three-step discovery sequence: *What is lost? What is left? What is possible?*

There are themes within and across these successions which at times ascend in importance and at other times are less important. These themes can overlap and complement each other, or at times even contradict each other."

    –John M. Schneider, *Finding My Way*

death. When they ask to speak to him, I have this strange temptation to turn and call him to the phone in the way I've done for all those years of our marriage."

This time involves the need to acknowledge that something is missing and to find ways to cope while gradually discovering the extent of the loss. Addressing our losses typically involves the struggle between acknowledging the full impact without having that awareness overwhelm or destroy us. During this time, we flow back and forth between the initial extremes of making too much of what we have lost and minimizing it. The actual truth is somewhere in between these two extremes, and that is what answering this first question is about.

Stanley shared these comments after the company where he worked for over fourteen years closed its doors. "Weeks after the closing, I'm still finding new losses that are a result of my job loss. I'm beginning to realize how much of my identity and self-esteem were wrapped up in my job as division head. I've lost so much more than my source of income! It seems like every day I discover one more thing that's gone. I know I have to get busy seeking another job, but right now I just don't have the energy for it."

Figure 1-1:
Discovering What is Lost

LOSS

Grieving Begins

Coping

Holding On ⟷ Letting Go

Active Grieving

AWARENESS

Significant Assumptions
Challenged by Loss

I am responsible.
I am not responsible.

I can only live moment to moment.
I will live on indefinitely.

I can control anything important to me.
No matter how hard I try, I am helpless.

I will always find something meaningful in life.
There's no real future for me.

I can count on things staying the same.
I can't count on anything or anybody.

Justice and fairness will ultimately win out.
Justice and fairness don't exist.

Everything has a purpose and a meaning.
Life ultimately has no purpose or meaning

This is the best of times.
This is the worst of times.

I am different from everyone else in the world.
I'm just like everybody else.

Someone will take care of me.
No one cares about me.

Coping with loss...
*~ from John M. Schneider's **Finding My Way***

Significant losses can be overwhelming. We can't take in their entire meaning at one time. We need times of respite and delay when we can focus on other things, and maintain and rebuild our lives. We need to know how to cope, to eventually get back on our feet. Our ways of coping are characterized by strategies that limit our awareness of loss: we hold on (fight) and we let go (flight). In some ways, we try to live only in our best self (holding on) or totally without it (letting go). Eventually, our sense of integrity will bring us together, able to measure the full extent of what we've lost.

Holding On / Beliefs and Myths

If I don't concentrate on remembering what has happened, I'll forget it.

If I work hard enough, nothing bad will ever happen to me.

If I'm good enough, nobody I love will ever die.

Cheer up – things could be worse!

It will all work out in the long run.

If I can understand why it happened, everything will be all right.

Every cloud has a silver lining.

It's God's will. He has something special in mind.

People get the respect they deserve in this world.

Don't question it, just accept it. You have to go on.

The show must go on.

I must learn to accept it.

Idle hands are the devil's workbench.

There must be a reason for this.

If I am good enough or perfect, what I lost will come back.

Letting Go / Beliefs and Myths

Eat, drink and be merry, for tomorrow may never come.

Why get involved? You just get hurt.

It's God's will. Learn to accept it.

Nobody cares about me. Why should I care about anybody else?

Easy come, easy go.

There's no such thing as a free ride.

I'm better off without him.

The good die young.

Out of sight, out of mind.

What the eye doesn't see, the heart doesn't remember.

What did I tell you? You can't trust anybody.

It's best to forget it. There's nothing you can do about it.

If you're too happy, something bad will happen.

Fate is against me.

To succeed is to die.

Don't settle for less than perfection.

Varieties of Loss

The key factor in grief is the degree of <u>attachment</u> that we had for that which is lost. The attachment need not be a positive one – it may even have been negative or conflicted. This is why some people grieve the very person or thing they disliked.

Other factors that are important to understanding our grief or that of others:

❖ Most losses have secondary aspects that also, then create grief, i.e., Susan's husband's death also meant she no longer had someone to tell about her day each evening.

❖ Grief will be affected by whether the loss was anticipated or unexpected.

❖ Grief will also differ depending on the degree of choice the grieving person had in the loss. One of the biggest issues in coping with a loss is the loss of control over one's circumstances or the loss factors.

❖ There are both internal and external aspects of loss.

Many people expect a bereaved person to be at "What's Possible" in their journey through grief, without understanding that they need to spend time with "What's Lost" and "What's Left."

Some losses are fairly obvious and typically understood by society as a loss. With these, it is expected that there will be grief (i.e., the death of a child). Other losses are more difficult to recognize for the elements of loss contained in them (i.e., a child taken from a "bad" parent). Still others may be seen only as positive events while the loss aspect is unrecognized (i.e., the birth of a healthy, normal baby). People in these situations may be ignored or even scorned for any sad feelings. There is a table of these types of losses on page 11.

It's a kind of test...and it's the only kind that amounts to anything. When something rotten like this happens, then you have your choice. You start to really be alive, or you start to die. That's all.

~ James Agee, A Death in the Family (1957)

Varieties of Loss

Obvious Losses:

*Death of a spouse, partner or other
    loved one*
Death of a child
Stillbirth
Miscarriage
Divorce
Separation
Illness
Chronic illness
Disability

Theft
Destruction of property
Moving
Buying/selling valued objects

Loss of a dream
Relationship ending

Job layoff
Job change

Loss as part of change:

Maturation
Relationship maturation
Aging
Loss of Memory

Weaning
Puberty changes

Leaving home
Child leaving home
Starting school

Positive Events:

Being in love
Marriage
Birth of a child

Wealth
Fame
Winning a prize

Mastering a new skill
Forming new relationship
Graduating or finishing school
Ending therapy

Job promotion
Business success
Project completion
Retirement

Collective Losses:

Natural disaster
Loss of shelter, food or safety

Organizational Losses:

Company closing
Company re-organization
Business failure

Internal Aspects of Loss   — *from John M. Schneider's* **Finding My Way**

There are aspects of our lives that we define as essential to being alive. These include what gives our life meaning – our values, our beliefs, our way of being. Losses can challenge this essence. We may lose a sense of connection to anything and anyone. The resulting feeling of loneliness challenges our spirituality, our willingness to reach out, to believe in our "best self," and to place hope in powers stronger than the forces beating us down. If a loss is severe enough, we may even decide that life is not worth living.

It is obvious that our spiritual well-being can be disrupted when our belief system is challenged. Validating spiritual losses is important if we are to grieve them. Without grief, we have no capacity to discover a more mature and robust spirituality that fits our present circumstances and helps us understand the new – and old – meaning in our lives.

There are challenges that everyday life makes on our values and our will to live. Our will to live is a compilation of all the forces within us – our mind, body and spirit – that determines what it takes for us to survive. With every significant loss, a spiritual question is asked: *Is there enough left to keep going?* We may think we know the answer only to discover that life has something else in mind for us.

Sometimes we go on when it makes no sense to do so – living in pain, fear, humiliation, poverty, illness. Years later, we may find our suffering has given us a depth, a credibility, and a message of hope for others and ourselves. But some lose their spirit while continuing to exist physically. One definition of depression is *the loss of a spiritual self.*

The loss of assumptions is, in a way, a loss of innocence. To function in life, we take many things for granted, including assumptions, prejudices and routine ways of behaving. A loss may force us to examine and discard these old ways. We lose our innocence.

Losses threaten assumptions. In some instances, such as a "mid-life crisis," every presumption or belief we have seems invalid and disrupts the way we view our world. They change the way we behave, adding another set of losses.

What is LEFT?

This next question involves opening ourselves to that which we have left after the loss. This is the time when our senses begin to reawaken to experiences other than or outside of the loss. We begin to consider other aspects of our life and discover which of those have been less impacted by the loss.

Josh, whose daughter died of acute leukemia at age 12, said, "The other kids, my son age 8, and my other daughter, age 10, keep me busy with all their activities. It's not like they replace Cindy – we all miss her terribly - but it's nice to go to one of Eric's ball games and be reminded that I have other wonderful people in my life."

Figure 1-2:
Discovering What is Left

Once we have explored the extent of our loss and can still go on, healing begins. During this time we realize that we can return to our sources of support. Or we may even have discovered or developed new resources for nurturance that helped us make it through the darkest and most vulnerable times. We certainly still remember what we have lost, but also now begin to restore what we can. We can focus somewhat on those other pieces of our life again.

Jeremiah was struggling with the early signs of Alzheimer's when he said, "It's helpful to know that what is happening has a name now – Alzheimer's. As terrible as this is, it still gives me a way to make sense and make what is happening more predictable. Before I had the diagnosis, I thought I was losing my mind – emotionally, I mean. As frightening as losing my memory is, it's better now to know what it is."

In this time, we allow the meaningful aspects of that which remains in our lives to be remembered, even recognized. We now find ways to contain the loss, not simply limit our awareness of it.

The tasks during this part of the grief process can be exhausting and can be quite time-consuming. We may find we have very little energy.

Several years after her son, then age 15, was hit by a car while crossing a street, Patricia said, "It is just in the last few months that I have realized that Kevin has recovered all the functions he will ever regain after his accident. He is always going to need help with certain things and will only be employable in jobs doing simple tasks. This is really tough to face, but now I must get busy arranging for all that he will need in order to live as independently as possible. Then, maybe, I will begin to get back to my reading group and see more of my friends."

The honesty of awareness brought about as we contemplate all that was lost now gives way to the truth-seeking of perspective. For perspective to emerge, we need to want objectivity and openness. We need to accept our vulnerability brought on by the realization that we are not totally protected from having a loss. And, we need to also remember the way that it was.

In answering these first two questions, we then ask: Does enough remain? Is enough recoverable? If not, then what? Is it the end of life as we once knew it? Is being a permanent victim our role? Some will choose just to accept and adjust to their losses. Others will choose ways to grow from their losses. This last choice involves risk, knowing that life is fragile and success has no guarantees. It can also mean accepting that all we can be sure about is what we have right now – in this present moment.

Two years after her husband died, Alayne commented: "There has to be more to life than this. I can't accept that I'm supposed to sit back and live off his pension. My life has to have meaning once again. Yes, I can be hurt. That's a price I'm willing to pay."

It's exhilarating to be alive in a time of awakening consciousness; it can also be confusing, disorienting & painful.
–Adrienne Rich, "When We Dead Awake: Writing as Re-Vision," On Lies, Secrets & Silence (1978)

Having accepted the reality of the loss and the limits of what we have left, we take on tasks that include the discovery of life's potentials. Some people, with little or no opportunity to improve the quality of their life, choose to die or, at least, not to prolong life. This can be a valid choice for some. Clark, a young client with AIDS, demonstrated this choice when he said, "I've changed my motif from dying with AIDS to living as fully as I can with it."

It is at this time in the grief process that people often undergo some type of rite of passage (i.e., saying goodbye, finishing business, etc.) as a test of their commitment to growth. In doing so, it is not uncommon to find people doing things with others who can bear witness to their process such as having a personalized memorial service or a special graduation.

Joachin gathered his friends for a 'divorce party' many months after his wife walked out. He said, "People send out announcements for a birth, a wedding, and even a death. But a divorce is just as much a life-changing event as any of these. I was finally ready to clean the house – get rid of the rest of her things – and begin moving my life forward. I needed to formally acknowledge that with this event." Joachin created an event that became a "rite of passage" for him.

On the cusp between "What's lost" and "What's possible" is the process of integrating the loss into the fabric of life. Integrating loss is the hardest part of grief, for it involves rebuilding and restoration. It also requires forgiveness as well as relinquishing the role of victim.

Each of these is a difficult accomplishment, thus making this the place in grief where the most "work" is. We sometimes speak of the "tasks of grief" and this is the point in the process where we most clearly understand why we might use the term "task." This is the place in grief that involves work!

What makes it worth all the effort, grace and courage to go beyond the peaceful acceptance of the loss – to do this "work"? Is it the desire of some to make meaning of the loss – to go beyond simply putting this behind us? And even more interesting, is the fact that most approaches to grief describe this as the last part of the process, not a point somewhere in the "middle" of a complete transformation.

This third discovery of grief can best be described by the question, "What is possible?" Time spent with this question involves moving away from a focus on limitations. It is a period when we begin to broaden our perspective – admitting a range of new possibilities – and these ever widening. This is often a time of relinquishing old patterns. And this may also mean the loss of friends and loved ones who are willing to be present during hard times, but are frightened or mystified by our desire to move on.

Arlene and Jack experienced this when they left their support group for bereaved parents ten years after the death of their son: "When we left, no one from that group ever came to see us again. We weren't supposed to ever get over Tony's dying. It was as if they thought Jack and I had betrayed him – and them too."

The central focus of this point in the process is reformulation – focus on new things or old things with a "new eye". Self-empowerment also becomes a pivotal theme now.

Remaining solely focused on what is lost, one remains a victim. In contrast, a survivor's perspective is focused on "that which keeps us going". This third question, then, is a clear shift to survivorship.

When the question "What's Possible?" is asked, it is addressing the possibilities created out of this loss – not its limits, nor simply ways to continue in spite of the loss. In other words, what can happen because of the loss.

After a divorce at a young age, and the death of two subsequent spouses, Sylvia, now age 52, stated, "I sure wouldn't wish for any of these losses, but I find I have discovered some strengths within – I must be a survivor! This realization is giving me the courage to now change my career from book-keeping to museum management. This is something I've always wanted to do, but felt it was too risky. I've even gone back to school and now am doing an internship at our local art museum!"

At this point in grief, we are not yet what we will become, but we are getting there. We've gone beyond that which we have left to now consider possibilities. This may mean opening to connections that defy our senses and sensibilities.

The Chinese symbol for "crisis" is the combination of two symbols: one for "danger," the other for "opportunity."

Lee, a woman who lost a child and had several miscarriages, later described this period of time in these words, "Those losses, and the time I had to think and feel, led me to open to a bigger world, one that acknowledged suffering and death in a way that made living worthwhile."

In order to contemplate possibilities, however, we must abandon our search for the ONE right answer – or the best way! Reformulating loss emancipates us from focusing on limitations.

This is an active time in the grief process. It involves turning some possibilities into probabilities and some dreams into realities. All we have to do is accept the risks that sometimes the dream won't become a reality and that taking chances doesn't always pay off.

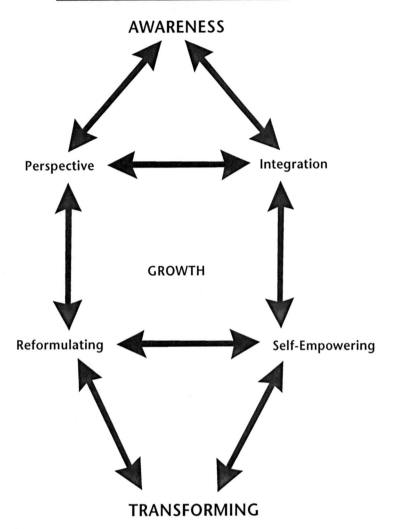

Figure 1-3:
Discovering What is Possible

AWARENESS

Perspective   Integration

GROWTH

Reformulating   Self-Empowering

TRANSFORMING

"**O**ften transformation requires altering the ways we look at the world. This process of reformulating and re-exploring means that we choose to risk loss and give up comfortable resolutions because we know that it is necessary for our own empowerment... Transformation that results from grieving can be characterized by a shift from limits to opportunities.

Transforming loss allows us to discover new ways to relate, understand, create and commit ourselves to an ongoing process of renewal and discovery. We come to know that loss, grief and the potential for transformation are parts of the cycle and the celebration of life. The knowledge permits us to grieve with less resistance and fear as we encounter new losses."

– John M. Schneider, *Finding My Way*

Transformative Grief

Loss and the subsequent grief are both universal experiences. Every one of us experiences loss at some point in our lives. And, the resulting grief is, perhaps, the most frequent path toward growth – even transformation. It is our responses to these losses, traumas, and even some successes that provide examples of what transformation is all about.

The word "transformation" means a significant alteration in the form of something – it is a moving across or beyond the old form to something unknown or unknowable before the change began.

In its healthiest sense, transformation is opening to a larger reality than the one our personal ego could admit previously. During the process of transformation, we experience being broken or of breaking with the past. We sense discontinuity in our lives as we go through any major transitions. That sensing of discontinuity, the healing that begins with acknowledging change, is an important part of the transformative journey we often call grief.

In spite of broken appearances, we aren't really changing what is meaningful to us. The essence of whom and what we are remains—the thread that weaves its way through our story. This thread remains unbroken despite our fears and concerns that this too is gone or broken. It is this fear of losing "ourselves" that means that typically, early in our grieving process we don't want to consider that we might grow or change as a result of moving through this process. Yet moving through this process is exactly what can eventually culminate in a positive outcome – even a transformation.

Transformation that results from grieving can be characterized by a shift from limits to opportunities. Transforming loss allows us to discover new ways to relate, understand, create, and commit ourselves. This can lead to an ongoing process of renewal and discovery. We come to know that loss, grief, and the potential for transformation

> *One word frees us of all the weight & pain of life: That word is Love.*
> *–Sophocles, Oedipus at Colonus*
> (cc. 406 BC)

are parts of the cycle of life – even the celebration of life. It is this knowledge that permits us to grieve with less resistance and fear as we encounter new losses. And certainly, whether we believe in an afterlife or not, we can more fully appreciate the value of contemplating it.

Ted lost the use of the lower half of his body while working under a car when the jack suspending it gave way. Years after rehabilitation and re-structuring his life so he could manage from a wheelchair, he readily says, "If I could get the full use of my legs and body back, but had to give up all I've gained – all the ways that I've grown, I wouldn't do it." *Ted has found a strong deep spirituality that not only became his strength in the grueling months of his "recovery," but which radiates from him, magnetically drawing others. He now has learned to pilot airplanes, and takes children with disabilities for airplane rides. He says, "I can't walk, but I can fly" – a literal statement which also symbolizes his own inner strength and the broadening of his life and awareness.*

What we have once enjoyed we can never lose. All that we love deeply becomes a part of us.
−Helen Keller,
We Bereaved (1929)

When experienced completely, transformation often requires altering the ways we look at the world. This process of reformulating and re-exploring means that we choose to give up our comfortable resolutions, even risking further losses, because we know that it is necessary for our own empowerment.

*In writing the original version of this book (**Finding My Way**), John shares some of his own story. "Early in my career as a psychologist, I did not want to let my clients face their "awareness" alone. Then, one of my intensive psychotherapy clients committed suicide out of depression, not grief. A few years later, twice I came close to death myself. Next, I went through a divorce. I left for Denmark, determined to reject what others needed from me. Then, overseas, I was shunned so completely I lost faith in myself.*

"After each of my personal losses, I became a little more honest about my limits and myself. Paradoxically, I became more capable of staying with people through the coping period and of respecting their need for privacy in awareness.

People who cannot feel punish those who do.
−May Sarton,
Mrs. Stevens Hears the Mermaids Singing (1965)

"Finally I realized that none of us could make it alone. We need to believe in something greater than ourselves in order to go on. I could have chosen to die – not by suicide, but by a lack of will to go on. Instead of dying, I found the love and hope I needed. I felt my own forgiveness and eventually believed I deserved to be loved. I recognize now that I'd been transformed each time I had a loss. I know the future holds more transformations for me, although I can't know the form they will take or when there won't be enough left for me to live for."

We can be present for others when our own life experiences have softened our defenses, taught us humility, given us patience and helped us recognize how important it is to experience awareness, to feel the full extent of being lonely, empty or helpless.

VALIDATION

What is it that we need during grief? What can be helpful in getting us through this process? What does the grieving person need from others? What might a loved one, a friend, or even a colleague, offer to someone who is dealing with a loss?

Validation is one of the most powerful tools for helping someone in grief. For most people there is tremendous relief in authenticating their losses. Grieving is a familiar process once we understand that we have experienced a loss and that we are in grief – a very normal reaction. Even when we acknowledge significant losses in our lives, we often feel we have no right to grieve, let alone to move on from the loss. The failure to recognize a loss makes it difficult to understand the resulting process of mourning. Simple validation, sometimes from others and sometimes from self, can be powerful in moving us through our grief. The more validation we receive, the stronger we become in facing our areas of greatest vulnerability and weakness. Validation can provide us with strength, especially when it acknowledges the reality and the fullness of the experience of our loss.

Some losses are of a nature that is difficult to support – even to recognize. Those that involve unpopular or antisocial behaviors or the breaking of social taboos can be like that.

For example, families often discredit the losses of a member who admits incest and thereby violates the family secrecy rule.

The chart below lists some of these.

Shared joy is double joy. And shared sorrow is half sorrow.
– Swedish proverb

Losses Difficult to Validate

Complicated	Controversial	Long-lasting	Chosen (when choice is available)
Divorce	Murder	Chronic illness	Abortion
Birth of a child	Insanity	Lifesyle change	Marriage
Child custody	Abuse	Death of a child	Promotion
Death of ex-spouse/0	Torture		Job resignation
ex-family member	Taboo		Moving
	Incest		Divorce
	Rape		
	Life-threatening illness		
	Losses due to sexual orientation		

When we are grieving, "staying with the moment" means knowing the fullness of *what we have lost*, so that we can appreciate *what is left,* know what needs to be restored and what we can then do with the *resulting possibilities.* Not experiencing the fullness of our losses either invalidates the remainder of the process or leaves incomplete our awareness of its meaning and its transformative potential.

As we conceptualize grief as a process, these three simple discovery questions are related to three different outcomes of validation: *to remember* (what's lost), *to restore* (what's left) and *to recreate* (what's possible). To feel validated in grief and hence, empowered toward healing, we must feel the safety to express our deepest thoughts and feelings, knowing that we will not be judged. We need to feel truly understood by those who witness our process. It is only then that we can begin to believe in our ability to be our best self. What is needed most is validation that things are as bad as they seem. The more fully a grieving person can accept that reality, the more likely it is they will find within themselves what it takes to go on.

The more we are validated, the more our self-esteem is enhanced. The more self-esteem we have, the more we are able to open to an awareness of our needs. The more self-aware, the more empowered we become to meet our needs physically, emotionally and spiritually. The more empowered we feel, the more we can consider the esteem needs of others, and the circle widens.

Loss & Therapeutic Validation
from John M. Schneider's **Finding My Way**

Loss can pervade any life experience. Recognition and support of the reality of a loss are essential for grief – the mechanism we have for renewal – to take place. Losses can be disenfranchised by families and society. We often fail to recognize significant losses because we lack safety and validation – from our family, friends or our culture... We learn to recognize when our beliefs are based on faulty or no longer valid premises.

From validating the extent and the limit of our losses, we gain an appreciation of what we have lost and what we have left. From expressing our grief, we gain motivation to live fully, and the zest for celebrating life's moments of success, pleasure and transformation. We can affirm life's worth and our appreciation for the opportunities we still have.

To validate, we need to believe: ❖ The person is capable of handling reality. ❖ They are doing the best they can at the present time. ❖ Their way of coping is appropriate to the complexities and stressfulness of the loss. ❖ Within them lies the strength for choices about their grief.

The table below provides an overview of validation as it applies to grief and healing:

Principles of Validation

PRINCIPLE	KEY POINTS
Commit to Empowering the Best Self	*Believe in the inherent worth, dignity and integrity of all individuals.* *Believe in an individual's ability to rise to the occasion.* *Believe that there is more to people than what "meets the eye."*
Appreciate the Moment & the Journey	*Live the moment fully.* *Savor the journey and the process.* *Honor sacredness.*
Witness the Moment & the Processs	*Hold hope.* *Be present at significant times.* *Share in an ongoing story.*
Be Gentle, with Honesty & Find Abiding Truths	*Be sensitive to communication dilemmas* *Commit to gentleness of the moment and truth of the process.*
Suspend Judgment	*Help to create emotional & spiritual safety.* *Know & respect your own values.* *Acknowledge differing viewpoints* *Temporarily set aside perspectives that are not helpful in the moment.*

WHAT IS GRIEF?

All change brings both gains and losses. As has been stated here, grief is the normal response to any major life change – good and bad, positive and not so positive. When we experience a significant change in our relationships and in our everyday lives – or if our worst nightmares become real – we may feel that our life story is broken or we have somehow fallen off the path we thought we were on, or even that life has become meaningless.

Our attachments, beliefs, and anchors to our past are no longer stable. We feel lost. The path before us no longer is clear or predictable. Life as we have known it may be over. Our current reality fills us with lonely, helpless, empty, and loveless times. We fear we've lost a significant part of ourselves – our best self – along with everything else. Our lives feel broken, transformed into a living nightmare.

Paradoxically, we can also experience such breaks when we are successful. Our accomplishments, love, or luck daze us. They seem too good to be true – and they are too good to last forever. Still, mastery, loving attachments, and fortune can create discontinuity with our past. We may have fame, possessions, pleasure, wealth, and security we never dreamt possible. We hope we've lost contact with our old selves – the parts of us that were ordinary, often helpless, and incompetent. Yet, our lives feel changed beyond recognition.

Priscilla had worked most of her adult life to create and build an organization, which could help women-owned small businesses. Now leading this organization with a staff of 11 people and with chapters in over 400 cities across the globe, she expected to feel a heady sense of accomplishment. Instead she found herself feeling empty inside – hollow – on most days. She said, "It's as if I have lost a dream instead of gaining it. It doesn't make sense to my closest loved ones because they see the outer successes – they just can't understand – and most of the time, neither can I. But for so many years my passionate drive was aimed at accomplishing this – now I have no new goals to energize me."

What has happened? Is it a sign of our "sinfulness" that bad things happen to us? Conversely, why do we not feel totally happy with what are supposed to be good changes? The answer is that all major life changes contain both gains and losses, and these need to be recognized, validated, and the losses grieved.

GRIEF DIFFERS FROM DEPRESSION

Grief is a normal, healthy, healing, and ultimately transforming response to a significant loss that usually does not require professional help, although it does require finding ways to heal the broken strands of life and to affirm existing ones. Grief can be the start of being fully alive!

The word "grieving" suggests that it is possible to know why we feel low, for grief is tangible – the direct result of the loss aspect of any change. When we are grieving, we know there is a connection – we are struggling with how to recognize its extent and limits, embrace its significance, remember it and restore its meaning. To call what we are feeling "grief" powerfully validates – makes real – our losses, our grief and our potential to transform it.

Through grieving we can gain the courage to do what we need to do. We find strength we didn't know we had because we had to. We face limits and find new options. We face dark parts of ourselves and know that forgiveness is necessary for continued life. We discover we can't make it all on our own.

Depression, on the other hand, represents a state of disconnection that can be the result of a biological, psychological, spiritual, or even circumstantial imbalance that makes it impossible to function fully after a loss. You begin to just exist, and, in the extreme, only are alive until death itself provides the release. Depression is the inability to grieve, either temporarily or permanently.

When we feel depressed, it is because we cannot or resist finding reasons or connections that would "fit" with what we feel. In fact, depression often disappears when we find such a connection. Depression is something to survive, to cope with, or to defend against, but it is not a condition in which we can learn new methods of coping or transform old ones. Depression is frequently vague and fuzzy, and so are our problems and the way to health, wholeness and reconnection.*

And yet we live in a world that uses the term depression to describe most negative feelings of sadness. It is most unfortunate that even grief is frequently called depression, as these two states are very different. Even health professionals, including mental health, frequently label and treat grief as if it were depression.

In fact, the way to deal with grief is exactly the opposite of the best response for depression. Grief and depression take us down very different paths.

---

*More information on this can be found in John Schneider's book: *The Overdiagnosis of Depression* (Seasons Press, 2000). This book also includes a diagnostic tool.

People who are depressed usually require professional help to further avoid or limit this "illness," whereas those who are grieving most need permission to grieve and legitimization that, in fact, they've had a loss. In other words, they need validation. Even the medications given for depression can inhibit grief. And currently, insurance companies don't reimburse for health care provided due to grief.

Grief transforms while depression deforms. In short, when we are grieving, we can consider both despair and hope, though perhaps not at the same moment. In depression, hope neither exists nor is sought. Consequently, while grieving responds to the love and support that a healing community can provide, depression usually requires professional help to contain, limit, or alter its potentially devastating impact. Only on limited occasions (perhaps thirty percent of the time) does grieving get so complicated that it requires grief counseling or other forms of professional support.

The bereaved person can move through the natural flow of the grieving process – through the process of discovery as shared here by the three questions: 1) What is lost? 2) What is left? 3) What is possible? The depressed person cannot make the shift from *What's Lost?* to *What's Left?* They are lost in *What's Lost?*

See the charts on pages 29–30 for a comparison of some of the differences between these two conditions.

There is a third path that is often in between the other two: feeling discouraged. To be "discouraged" literally means something has "dissed" our courage. So the issue is finding courage, rather than giving in to the stresses. Discouragement results from many circumstances that create complications that seem like depression: being arrested, sued for malpractice, fired from a job, or being raped all combine a sense of shame and lost self-esteem. At the very least, we are traumatized and discouraged, the grief that results is complicated, and many of the losses can be disenfranchised (meaning "not validated") as well.

Depression only comes when these discouraging circumstances are met with a "depressed" response, such as giving up, giving in, or permanently accepting the role of victim. Certainly that can happen when those circumstances last for a long time and when those who are supposed to be sources of hope and recovery (such as family, friends, and counselors) actually contribute to the problem and lack of hope.**

**See more on discouragement in *Dying to Live or Living to Die?* by John M. Schneider, PhD (Seasons Press, 2005).

If you try saying to yourself "I feel discouraged" instead of "I feel depressed" at such times and find that it works, you are probably not depressed – just discouraged, disheartened, or demoralized. At such times, what you need is to find courage, listen to your heart, and to reestablish your moral core.

Feeling discouraged makes sense when ailments aren't treated effectively or when we're told we have to "rely on our coping mechanisms." This is the case with many chronic illnesses, as well as accidents or injuries that permanently alter our body structure. But lots of things can discourage us, from unrelenting miserable weather to natural catastrophes, to accidents, to traumatic occurrences.

Feeling discouraged also makes sense when everybody else is going through the same thing. Whether it's boot camp, law school, or any other overwhelming job or training, everyone seems to share the experience. We can't complain because no one else does – or dares to.

Among other circumstances which can produce discouragement are:

❖ When it isn't safe to show feelings such as women in abusive relationships who keep returning to the abuser as if nothing had happened.

❖ When nobody considers what has happened as worthy of grieving such as when a favorite pet has died.

❖ When there's no time for self-exploration such as situations where life itself is so demanding that there's literally no time or energy to grieve.

❖ When our support systems have dried up.

❖ When life itself is extremely stressful.

Facilitating Grief's Transformations
from John M. Schneider's **Finding My Way**

There are several key elements which, if fulfilled, help people find a transformative path through their grief:

❖ *The need to feel cared for, secure, protected and loved;*

❖ *The need for validation of reality at times of transition and loss;*

❖ *The need for challenge when a loss becomes our only important identity;*

❖ *The need for facilitative environments – places of sanctuary and therapeutic communities;*

❖ *The need for play and humor to have a role in the healing pocess;*

❖ *The need to ultimately find a source of nurturance, validation, forgiveness and adventure from within.*

KEY DIFFERENCES BETWEEN GRIEF & DEPRESSION
A thumbnail sketch, not to be used as a comprehensive clinical assessment tool.
(based on passages from John Schneider's "Finding My Way")

ISSUE	GRIEF	DEPRESSION
Is there a loss?	Yes.	Maybe/maybe not.
What do they think about?	At times, they may be obsessed with the loss. At other times, they can think of other things.	Often obsessed with themselves and how this loss is unfair or a punishment
What are their dreams & fantasies?	Vivid, clear dreams, sometimes of the loss, which can sometimes be comforting.	Flashbacks, nightmares, same disturbing dreams over & over.
What is the physical effect?	Gains or loses some weight. Exercises a lot or stops entirely. Has trouble getting to sleep. Feels tired a lot.	Weight change is extreme. Exercise is also at extremes. Has trouble waking up, awakens with disturbing dreams. Always restless or always sleepy or tired.
What is the spiritual effect?	A connection is felt to something beyond the self, e.g., a belief in God and that this is happening for a reason. Able to challenge, revise, or maintain previously held beliefs.	Especially a year or more past a loss, a persistent failure to find meaning and a continued focus on "Why me?" or the unfairness & meaninglessness of the loss. Resists any "pat" answers when they question beliefs. Tends to discard previously held beliefs.
How do they feel?	Moody. Shifts in mood from anger to sadness to more positive feelings in the same day.	Can be hard to "read" emotionally, or they can be at an extreme, either crying all the time or not at all, angry all the time or not at all. Rarely feels "good."
How do they respond to others?	Generally responds to warmth, pressure, and reassurance. They appreciate being left alone but not ignored.	Either can't stand people at all or can't be without them. They respond to promises and urging or they remain unresponsive. Often feels abandoned & unloved when alone.
What happens when having pleasurable experiences?	As long as the pleasure isn't something that only came from the loss (e.g., sex after losing partner), it can be OK.	Either extreme: "Eat, drink & be merry," or experience no pleasure at all.
How do they attach and relate to others?	Likes to have close friends or someone who will listen to their story. Misses being loved or able to love others.	Feels unloved and incapable of loving & often goes about proving it by distancing self from others.

TYPICAL BEHAVIORS of GRIEF & DEPRESSION

Grieving (but not depressed) people may:
❖ *Find dreams helpful*
❖ *Fear they are going crazy*
❖ *Admit their feelings scare them*
❖ *Say "I feel depressed"*
❖ *Never forget who or what they lost*
❖ *Respond to nurturance and support*
❖ *Find the courage to forgive and let go*
❖ *Admit they need help*
❖ *Be open to every consequence of a loss*
❖ *Be motivated to create new meaning in their lives*
❖ *Hope that things might get better someday*
❖ *Need validation that things are as bad as they seem*
❖ *Eventually be able to realize their wholeness comes out of that grief*
❖ *Say, "If I continue to feel this way, I'm not sure life is worth living."*
❖ *"Look good" six months after a loss even when they still don't feel good*
❖ *Choose not to go back to life before the loss occurred if it means giving up the growth resulting from their grief*

Depressed people may:
❖ *Be unable to forgive*
❖ *Be at risk for suicide*
❖ *Pray only for deliverance, not for strength*
❖ *Find their dreams repetitive and disturbing*
❖ *Refuse to talk about or acknowledge that loss*
❖ *Be unable to cry or unable to stop crying*
❖ *Avoid their feelings or constantly live in them*
❖ *Believe nobody cares and have developed ways to prove it*
❖ *Believe perfection is possible and that forgiveness is impossible*
❖ *Be unable to tolerate the good times and rain on other people's parades*
❖ *Dislike being touched or can never get enough touching (sex)*

Both Grieving and Depressed people may:
❖ *Lose or gain weight*
❖ *Have trouble sleeping*
❖ *Feel tired and exhausted*
❖ *Not want to be hurt again*
❖ *Avoid pleasurable activities*

Material taken from *The Overdiagnosis of Depression: Recognizing Grief and its Transformative Potential* by John M. Schneider, PhD (Seasons Press, 2000).

GRIEF IS A HOLISTIC PROCESS

Grief pervades our entire being following a significant loss. It will have an impact on our bodies, our emotions, our mind and our spiritual being. These multiple dimensions are the ways we experience the world. As a result signif icant losses involve all these aspects of our-selves: the ways we act (behavioral), how we think (cognitive), the feelings we have (emo-tional), the responses of our body (physical), and the meaning and values we have (spiritual). At each point in the grieving process there is an affect on each of these aspects of our being – each of which may differ from the impact of an earlier point or time during our grief. We may be profoundly aware of this or it may be less apparent – both to us as well as to oth-ers around us. Yet grief can affect every aspect of our lives and of ourselves.

The diagram we saw on page 7, "***The Themes of Grief***," shows how, in each of these dimensions: physical, emotional, spiritual, cognitive, and behaviorial, we will experience the various themes – each of the questions of the discovery process. Although not nec-essarily sequential, these themes will at times overlap and complement each other. And at other times, they may even contradict each other.

MEN AND WOMEN ARE LIKELY TO EXPERIENCE DIFFERENT WAYS OF GRIEVING

Men and women often misunderstand each other's grieving processes. Men are more likely to want to put the loss behind them quickly and to cope by being productive. Men tend to fear shaming – either by others or themselves. Women tend to be more open, emotive, and inclusive in viewing their loss. Because of the relative emphasis we place on our masculine and feminine characteristics, we may tend to see men as not grieving at all and women as grieving too much and too long. In reality both are grieving, but emphasizing different aspects of the process. These gender-differing strategies have developed in our culture over many decades, even centuries, and are a survival mechanism against stress and change.

OTHER IMPORTANT FACTS ABOUT GRIEF:

1 *The natural outcome of experiencing a significant loss is a <u>process</u> of grieving.*

As has been stated here, grieving is the natural consequence of losing something or someone we value; it is our way of adjusting to change. It is also important to note that as a process, it is likely to take time and to change in its manifestation at different points in the process. It may even seem to end, only to return.

2 *Grief is a <u>healing</u> process.*

Grief is a universal human reaction that allows us to recover fro m and even grow as a result of a loss. Healing can occur if external factors (validation, resources, and support) and internal factors (safety, ego strength, and flexibility in coping styles) are available.

3 *The loss of any significant attachment is a threat to <u>all</u> significant attachments, including our own life.*

We'd like to believe that a particular loss doesn't raise the possibility of other losses, but it does. Awareness means we'll look at every way this loss could affect us. As we face awareness, we may even fear that our very identity, who and what we are, will also be lost. If we are to reorder the priorities in our life, as often happens after a loss, we need to examine what those priorities are – including our commitment to life itself.

4 *We can't take in a loss all at one time.*

We don't take in the whole of our loss and its significance in a single moment, unless, of course, the loss is relatively minor. We're likely to make successive approximations to the true impact of the loss or to only take in a piece at a time. Life needs to go on in between the moments we spend in awareness.

5 *The ways we have dealt with previous changes in our lives will affect our reactions to current and future losses.*

Patterns of dealing with loss are handed down through family traditions, cultural legacies, and religious rituals. If we've feared or experienced abandonment earlier in our lives, losses escalate our separation anxieties. It's very hard to alter our responses, especially in the middle of a crisis – like trying to teach someone to swim while they are drowning. Yet it is possible to change our responses and to break with the limits placed on us by others or by our past experiences.

6 *We don't "get over" a significant loss, but we can move on.*

Grieving involves "abstracting what was fundamentally important about the loss and rehabilitating it." Instead of getting over what we lost, we incorporate its meaning and its memory into the fabric of the rest of our lives. Such integration and reformulation allows us to see growth potential in tragedy, learning in suffering, new direction in chaos, and continuity in change. Still, it takes some time to reach this theme in grief, often long after the time of painful awareness has passed.

DISCOVERIES & CHOICES, NOT STAGES & PHASES

Elizabeth Kübler-Ross, M.D. pioneered the recognition of loss and grief as important processes in our lives in her work and writing of her book *On Death and Dying*. In it, she proposed five stages of grief, from denial to anger to bargaining, depression, and acceptance.

While this was a major step toward understanding the processes of dying and of grieving at that time, we now understand more about the grieving process. As valuable as this pioneering work was, Kübler-Ross' five psychological states came to be understood and applied by the public (and by caregivers, in particular) in a way that created problems. Most notably, there was, and often still is, a strong tendency to regard the five stages as an inflexible sequence – grieving people should move through these stages at some prescribed pace or else they aren't "doing it right." In addition, acceptance, the final stage, is all that can be expected out of grieving, especially with one's own dying. In reality, people in grief do not go through a linear progression of grief stages as described above. Grieving is a process that has its ebbs and flows, ups and downs, exhilarating insights and plunges into the bottom of the pits.

The complexity of grief is now better understood than it was when Kübler-Ross began her work with the dying. It used to be that many caregivers ignored other grief responses unrelated to the dying process, as a sign of a pathological reaction. More recently, many have regarded the tendency to see anything more than these simple steps as signs that grief is getting complicated and therefore in need of professional help.

The work of Elizabeth Harper Neeld, author of *Seven Choices: Finding Daylight After Loss Shatters Your World* (Warner Books, 2003) has dealt with both death and divorce in her personal life, and suggests a series of existential choices that are made in grief that also suggest or lead to a transformative process.

Research on grief has revealed that people tend to include issues from all parts of their grief for many years as they go on with their lives. The relative emphasis shifts from what is lost through what is left to what is possible, but these questions still remain open to new information about the loss and a reactivation of the whole process. Grief is a process that involves choices and defining moments – and a sequence of questions that are asked over and over again.

GRIEF & SOCIETY

It is a myth of modern society that success in relationships, individual accomplishments, technology, fame, wealth, or knowledge can eliminate the necessity of grieving. We occasionally discard that myth, for example, in the process of surviving wars and natural disasters. People put aside their personal agendas to fight, shelter, shovel, and sandbag for collective survival. The World Trade Center bombing and the tragedies of September 11, 2001

And be not conformed to this world, but be ye transformed by the renewing of your mind.
–Romans 12:2

showed us how a society can pull together in a crisis, and all too vividly illustrated mass grieving. Remembering the impact of September 11, 2001, most of us know almost no one of our personal acquaintances who was unaffected by these events.

Individuals, communities, and nations who go through profound catastrophes are rarely the same afterwards. Old bonds are disrupted by war or drugs. When brother betrays brother, our attachments to family and childhood can be lost. Common adversity creates strange bedfellows. When our earthly possessions are destroyed, we have to look beyond the material to find a reason to go on living.

Whether it is a private or shared tragedy that cracks our fragile eggshell of individuality, we open to new, more inclusive definitions of what makes life worth living.

The loss of illusions and the discovery of identity, though painful at first, can be ultimately exhilarating and strengthening.
–Abraham Maslow, Toward a Psychology of Being (1958)

Everything that has a beginning has an ending. Make your peace with that and all will be well.
– The Buddha

CONCLUSION

FACING OUR GREATEST FEARS CAN BE LIBERATING

We can place our smaller fears in a larger context when we have faced our greatest fears – dying, loneliness, helplessness, loss of meaning and purpose – that can result from facing a significant loss. If we fear abandonment, for example, and someone important to us dies or leaves us, we are faced with the fulfillment of that fear. Grief allows us to mature in the process of facing fears. When we can face our greatest fears, they can no longer imprison us.

FIRST THE DARKNESS, THEN THE LIGHT

It is a peculiarly unique belief of the late twentieth century that people have "options" when it comes to loss, grief, death, and dying, meaning there is a belief that it is possible to go through life without really having to come to grips with reality. These beliefs generally involve one of three forms of selective consciousness. The first involves an emphasis on the survival capacity of human nature. The second involves the freedom from responsibility that comes from seeing oneself as a victim. And the third comes from the notion that people always have choices, including the choice to avoid suffering. People use this selectivity of awareness to create false alternatives to experiencing loss and grief.

To find deeper meaning in life one must consciously embrace three aspects of reality:

❖ Suffering exists and cannot be avoided without paying an even greater price;

❖ When suffering is validated, healing results;

❖ Suffering and healing renew possibilities for love and joy.

Addressing these aspects of reality is part of a larger process – the need to fully grieve the losses we encounter in life. Effective grieving insists that these challenges be addressed consciously and fully, as well as approached, rather than avoided or distorted.

Significant losses overwhelm. We can't take them in wholly at one time. We need time for coping (i.e., respite and delay), times when we can focus on other things, and maintain and rebuild our lives. We need to know how to cope, to eventually get back on our feet.

Grief waits for the time and place where safety and freedom from judgment exist, with someone who validates the reality of grief and supports the time it needs to heal. Without safety, validation, support and hope, we lack the essential ingredients to move on when we are stuck in even the most common of life experiences. We need freedom not to fear judgment and shame. We need to be convinced that our story won't hurt, devastate or alienate the other. We need to anchor our experiences with words, drawings, sculpture, poem and songs. We need to discover other people who have had similar, perhaps identical experiences to us – and have come through them. Validation of our pain is mandatory if this healing process is to begin and be passed on.

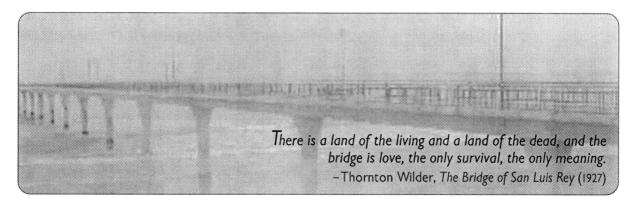

There is a land of the living and a land of the dead, and the bridge is love, the only survival, the only meaning.
–Thornton Wilder, *The Bridge of San Luis Rey* (1927)

Whether loss is shared or not, it is through discovering the interweaving of our life experiences with loss that we find the universal threads that give hope – the threads which tell us that by fully facing what we experience, we can know what we have lost, what we have left, and what is possible. And we discover just how intricate, extensive, and empowering our connections are. It is then that transformation in the best possible way occurs. Then we can move through life with lessened fear of future losses, knowing any loss can expand horizons.

As we move through the grieving process from any major life change, we never return to the way things used to be. We discover what is lost, what remains, and what is possible, as we move from coping and adjusting to the creation of major life transformations!

Loss happens to everyone who makes connections. We create and maintain continuing bonds with those we love who have died, and assist each other by helping to reinforce the human potential involved in healing. Hence, we are all connected to each other. Although the experience of grief is an individual process, we are never alone.

Opportunities for recovery and transformation come when we believe in ourselves. Grieving and recovery may not be easy, but they *can* be joyful.

Those things which help us to move through this process are:

- ❖ *Feeling cared for;*
- ❖ *Being validated for the reality;*
- ❖ *Seeking facilitative environments;*
- ❖ *Finding places of sanctuary;*
- ❖ *Building therapeutic communities;*
- ❖ *Including play & humor;*
- ❖ *Creating rituals of recognition & commemoration;*
- ❖ *Testing our limits;*
- ❖ *Forgiving & being forgiven;*
- ❖ *Learning new means of creative expression while grieving;*
- ❖ *Recognizing our strengths in surviving & moving through the process.*

In the short term, the transformative process through loss creates another cycle of loss and grief. It is that pebble dropped in a still pool that radiates waves throughout. Yet, with greater openness and the willingness to surrender more readily the necessity of structure in life, the energies released can create new strength. These energies can open to new wisdom and a capacity to experience new levels of awareness of life, cherishing uniqueness and separateness. It can aid people in discovering the depth and extent of the love and joy they can share in this lifetime and what lies beyond.

As energy and strength are recovered, people's dreams can open again to explore ways of viewing what was lost in a broader context than previously possible. Now, there really is no possibility, no matter how painful, that needs to be feared. This opening to the possible makes perspective and reformulating the loss feasible, so that exploring ways to view what has been lost in a broader context is possible. There is no possibility, positive or negative, that needs to be feared. The imaginative capacity of people lifts them from the valley of despair to a place where perspective can occur.

NEW POSSIBILITIES

Transforming loss into a fuller life is a gift. When you grow from a loss, you have created a deeper, more enduring sense of hope that the energies hell-bent

on destroying the world through greed, disease, envy, war, environmental destruction, and the like can be transformed. You now have the gift of knowing that if you can change, as you now have, other transformations also are possible. You have the gift of knowing there can be hope found in the face of despair – as is <u>discovered</u> through transformation. You now have the gift of remaining open to what's ahead – and even what's beyond. You now have the gift of knowing that there are discoveries beyond this moment that can make your life and experience richer and richer – that life and loss involve discoveries that ultimately are the greatest reward!

Thus, as we understand the direct link between change, loss and grief, we can more fully understand that whether small or large, the changes we face

> And be not conformed to this world, but be ye transformed by the renewing of your mind.
> –Romans 12:2

are likely to trigger a loss reaction (grief). That reaction or grief is natural and very normal. This, then leads us to and through a very natural process – a process that unfolds and changes with time and with movement. Understanding the normalcy of this means we can more readily accept our own grief response. And it means that we can also better understand and help those around us.

Now we can be reassured that we need not fear nor resist this response to changes – to losses. Maybe, just maybe, we can face these changes with greater courage. This also means that we can be more understanding, more supportive and more validating of those around us.

Validation is such a powerful tool for moving through the pain of our losses. It can make a difference in the experience of others in our worlds as they face losses – work colleagues, family members, friends, and acquaintances. As we understand the importance of this listening and validating, we can be more supportive of them. But also this means that we can offer this same validation to ourselves at difficult times. We can be self validating! We can be more accepting of our own process, even more patient.

We can move more readily through our grief with the confidence that our grieving is meaningful and effective. We can know that it will go somewhere and not be stuck in the same place forever. And we can trust that the "somewhere" will be a much more positive place. We don't have to listen to the messages of rejection that emerge – both from ourselves and from well-meaning others.

> *Transforming loss allows us to discover new ways to relate, understand, create and commit ourselves to an ongoing process of renewal and discovery...*
> – John M. Schneider, **Finding My Way**

At last we can realize that the grieving process that previously seemed so complex, is in fact, fairly simple. The three important questions shared here (What's Lost, What's Left, and What's Possible), may seem simplistic, but in fact they hold deep meaning and great power as we work through them. And we need not worry about what "phase" we are in, but simply keep focused on these discovery questions.

There now is a greater possibility that by better understanding each other and ourselves when we are in pain, that we will have created a more caring, understanding world. A greater possibility that this world can be a much safer place. This will certainly then be true when life is running smoothly, but even more importantly, the world will be a much safer, saner place when life is changing!

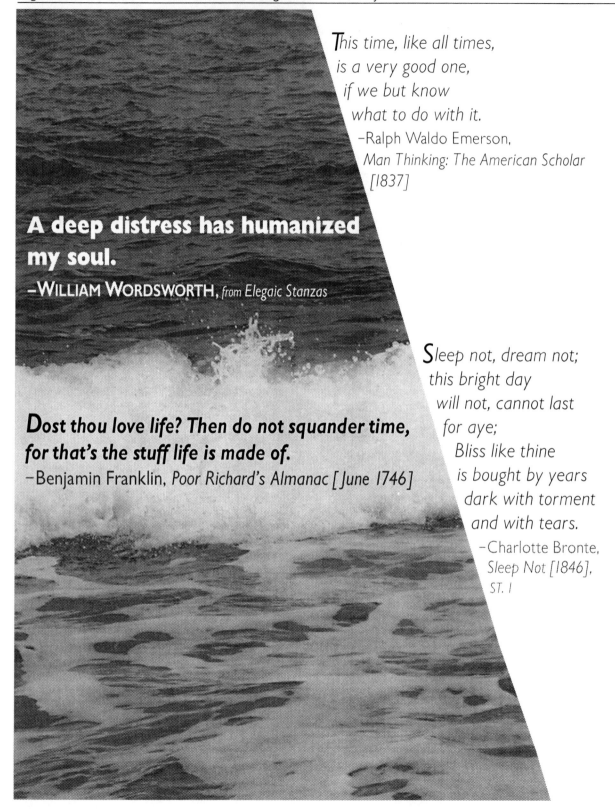

This time, like all times,
is a very good one,
if we but know
what to do with it.
 –Ralph Waldo Emerson,
 Man Thinking: The American Scholar
 [1837]

A deep distress has humanized my soul.
–WILLIAM WORDSWORTH, *from Elegaic Stanzas*

Sleep not, dream not;
this bright day
will not, cannot last
for aye;
 Bliss like thine
 is bought by years
 dark with torment
 and with tears.
 –Charlotte Bronte,
 Sleep Not [1846],
 ST. 1

Dost thou love life? Then do not squander time, for that's the stuff life is made of.
–Benjamin Franklin, *Poor Richard's Almanac* [June 1746]

About INTEGRA...

INTEGRA

The Association for Integrative and Transformative Grief

An international community of individuals dedicated to sharing the vision and value of transformative grief. Our basic philosophy is that grief & loss – when fully experienced – can positively transform lives.

This charitable non-profit organization works in the area of grief and loss, providing: ❖ newsletters ❖ speakers bureau ❖ arts programming ❖ workshops ❖ classes ❖ grief certification ❖ publications.

❖ EDUCATION ❖ RESEARCH ❖ SERVICE

Further information available at:
  http://www.integraonline.org
Or reach us at:
  P.O. Box 6013
  East Lansing, MI 48826
  Phone: (517) 339-7964
  E-mail: *szimmerman@integraonline.org*
Also, see John Schneider's articles on his website:
  http://www.seasonspress.com

Because we at INTEGRA plan other editions of this book, we would love to hear from you, our readers. *Send us your comments & stories.*

Watch for other versions of this book to be released soon:
  ❖ *eBook format*– *digital files downloadable to personal computers and portable eBook readers*
  ❖ *DBook format (floppy discs or CDs)*
  ❖ *ABook format (audiorecordings)*
  ❖ *Study course*

Meet the Authors

John Martin Schneider, Ph.D.

John Schneider is a Distinguished Professor Emeritus from Michigan State University's Colleges of Medicine, having taken an early retirement after being on the faculty for twenty-five years. In the ten years since, he has written several books on grief, developed a private practice that focuses on medical clinical psychology as it applies to issues of aging, illness, trauma, grief, depression, disability, restorative justice, life quality and dying, while also focusing on the creative skills that enhance living fully. He is a member of the International Work Group on Death, Dying and Bereavement (IWG). John continues to write both fiction and non-fiction, supervise, facilitate research using his grief instruments, consult internationally, and work in pastoral care in his religious congregation. John also has an educational website: *www.seasonspress.com*.

John is also co-founder of **INTEGRA: The Association of Integrative & Transformative Grief.**

Susan K. Zimmerman, M.S.

Susan is co-founder and president of Integra: The Association for Integrative & Transformative Grief and Loss, an international non-profit working in the area of loss and grief. She also is president of PASSAGES Transition Center, a consulting and coaching business working with organizations and individuals during times of transition. Retired from Michigan State University where she served on the central administration in many areas including the President's Office, she now is an educator and speaker on loss and change.

Among her honors are receipt of an honorary ATHENA award, given by the international board of the ATHENA Foundation; being featured in the book *When Money Isn't Enough: How Women are Redefining Success for the 21st Century*, by Connie Glaser & Barbara Smalley (authors of Swim with the Dolphins. Warner Books, 1998); as well as being honored by the Michigan House of Representatives and Senate in 1982 when they also recognized her with Senate Concurrent Resolution #803.

This book is a condensed version of
Finding My Way: Healing and Transformation
Through Loss and Grief
by John M. Schneider, PhD
Seasons Press, 1994

Other books by John Schneider:

Grief's Wisdom: *Quotes that Validate the Transformative Process*
by John M. Schneider, PhD   Season's Press   170 Pages   ISBN: 0-9638984-5-0
Schneider has compiled an anthology of quotations on loss and grief from a vast array of contributors throughout history. By illustrating how universal the process of grief is, he validates the transformative potential of grief. A companion volume to **Finding My Way**, this anthology is a wonderful resource for personal and professional use.

The Overdiagnosis of Depression: *Recognizing Grief and its Transformative Potential*
by John M. Schneider, PhD   Season's Press   160 Pages   ISBN: 0-9638984-4-2
Too often, the diagnosis of depression is given to persons who are more correctly grieving and the results can be profoundly damaging. Schneider addresses the differences between depression and grief, identifies how significant changes are losses to be grieved, assesses when professional help is necessary, and explores the benefits of a healing community. This book is suitable for professional and lay readers.

All of the above books are available online at **www.integraonline.org** or **www.seasonspress.com**.

Printed in the United States
45835LVS00004BA/3-536

9 780977 298006